PROCESS THEOLOGY AND PROPHETIC FAITH

I0191616

BRUCE EPPERLY

Energion Publications
Gonzalez, Florida
2023

ISBN: 978-1-63199-887-4
eISBN: 978-1-63199-888-1

Energion Publications
1241 Conference Rd
Cantonment, FL 32533

energion.com
pubs@energion.com

TABLE OF CONTENTS

CHAPTER ONE

PROPHETIC VISION

Let justice roll down like water
and righteousness like an ever-flowing stream.
(Amos 5:24)

Process theology is prophetic theology. Process theology charts the distance between the concrete realities of history, in all their wondrous diversity, conflict, and compassion, and the vision of what can be in a world where beauty, peace, adventure, and justice are the norm. Believing God to be embedded in the human and planetary adventure, process theology expresses divine restlessness at the way things are and confronts the injustice and violence of our daily interpersonal and institutional lives. While recognizing that God's aim is often the "best for that impasse" and that we must settle for incremental progress in the quest for human wholeness and institutional healing, it also shouts, "Glory, glory, hallelujah, God's truth is marching on."

Process theology grounds itself in the messiness of history: labor strikes, traumatizing of immigrant children, train derailments, gun lust, falling bombs, melting glaciers, book banning, and racist rhetoric. It also imagines the moral and spiritual arcs moving through history, motivated by the statement, "There are those who look at the way things are, and ask why. I dream of things that never were and ask, why not?" Always youthful, fresh, and hopeful despite the realities of institutional incivility and alienation, process theology embraces the "tragic beauty" of life and imagines the far horizons of a world in which the streets are filled with the laughter of children, friends, and family gather in peace for meals and celebrations, schools are places of safety and untrammeled imagination, and humankind prizes the power of love over the love of power.

I began this text on Ash Wednesday 2023, a day of prophetic confession and repentance, and completed my first draft during the Lenten season of repentance and sacrificial living. A

1

holy and prophetic season challenging us to examine our values and the distance between God's vision and the world in which we all-too-comfortably live. The ashes of mortality challenge us to affirm, "Now is the day of salvation," wholeness, transformation, and new life for us and our institutions. We have seen too much death, much of it the result of wayward and self-seeking institutions and nations, and we need to repent, turn around, and become God's partners in healing the earth. We need to see the world with God's transfigured mountaintop vision and then descend filled with God's healing presence into pits of despair, halls of incivility, and neighborhoods of hopelessness.

On Ash Wednesday and in the lengthening days of Lent, we affirm the prophetic spirit that announces that the world can change and that we can be God's partners in healing the planet. On Ash Wednesday and during Lent, and every season of the year, we awaken the penitent and prophet within, not just for forty days but for a lifetime. The voice of God within and around us, restlessly challenging the waywardness of our time and calmly moving beyond self-interest to world loyalty, motivated by the awareness that though we glimpse but a shadow, we can experience God's vision and incarnate that lively, restless, challenging vision.

Process theology is prophetic theology. Within each moment of experience, there is the vision of something more. Emerging from the realities of this moment, and its history and environment, process theology presents a lure for a wider vista, greater stature, and deeper beauty that stands in contrast with the values of our world. God's spirit marches on and invites us to "march in the light of God" and heal the earth and its peoples. Glory Hallelujah! This is the God of Amos and Hosea, John the Baptist and Jesus, Gandhi and Dorothy Day, Howard Thurman, Martin Luther King, Greta Thunberg, and Oscar Romero. The God of dreams and visions, hoping for a time in which all God's children gather together for celebrations, weather patterns stabilize, and nations study war no more.

Prophetic Vision. While there have been prophets throughout the ages, challenging the values of every social system on every continent, this text has its inspiration in the First or Old Testament prophets, who lived in a time of social and political upheaval, idolatry, and injustice, and called out political and religious leaders, the elite and privileged members of society, to embody God's vision of Shalom in their decision-making and business practices. This brief study is also motivated by the ministry of Jesus, whose first sermon embraced the prophetic vision of those Hebraic prophets:

> *The Spirit of the Lord is upon me,*
> *because God has anointed me*
> *to bring good news to the poor.*
> *God has sent me to proclaim release to the*
> *captives*
> *and recovery of sight to the blind,*
> *to set free those who are oppressed,*
> *to proclaim the year of the Lord's favor.*
> (Luke 4:18-19, AP)

Quoting the prophet Isaiah, Jesus preached the good news that God's Realm is near and calls for personal and national repentance. Imagining a new world order emerging among the marginalized and the elite, Jesus opened his arms to the dispossessed, unclean, forgotten, and downtrodden. He touched the outcast and inspired repentance among the powerful. Following his Parent's vision, Jesus prayed that God's realm come to pass "on earth as it is in heaven" (Matthew 6:10). A citizen of an oppressed land, never having lived a moment of freedom, Jesus taught a message of freedom which inspired his followers to transcend and transform the oppressive powers that encompassed them. Jesus enlisted his first followers to do greater things in embodying his all-inclusive, life-transforming ministry, and that challenge is ours today as we confront the growing impact of climate change, racism, anti-Semitism, economic injustice, incivility, division, sexism and heterosexism, and nuclear saber rattling, joined with the widening gap between the wealthy and impoverished.

The Prophetic Orientation. Process theology looks back to lean forward. The present and future moments emerge from the impact of our past history, both personal and political. Process theology embraces the past in its ambiguity, calling us to remember the pain as well as the hope of our predecessors and study the impact of the injustices our parents and nation perpetrated, or suffered, as decisive in shaping the present moment. We will look at two visions of the First Century prophets, articulated by Abraham Joshua Heschel and Walter Brueggemann, along with the spiritual vision of Dorothee Soelle, to help us chart the course of a lively process of prophetic faith.

Abraham Joshua Heschel's text, *The Prophets* finds its inspiration in the imagery of Divine Pathos, in which God "does not reveal himself in absolute abstractness, but in personal and intimate relationship to the world. He does not simply command and expect obedience; He is also moved and affected by what happens in the world and reacts accordingly. Events and human actions arouse in Him joy or sorrow, pleasure or wrath."[1] The Divine Pathos reflects God's commitment to finite, temporal, and creaturely existence. Similar to process theology, Heschel affirms that God hears the cries of the poor and feels the pain of the world. Embedded in history, the transcendent divinity needs humankind to achieve God's purposes. As Heschel claims, "the rabbis were not guilty of exaggeration in asserting, 'Whoever destroys a single soul should be considered the same as one who destroyed a whole world. And whoever saves one single soul should be considered the same as one who has saved a whole world.'"[2] The prophets see the world from God's perspective: God's pain at illness, injustice, and violence, much of which is the result of personal and institutional decision-making. The origin of the moral arc of history, Divine Pathos means that "God is never neutral, never beyond good and evil. He is always partial to justice."[3] According to Heschel, prophets do not predict the future, but are sensitive to the impact of institutional decisions in shaping a future that is open for God and us. If we change our ways, we may avoid catastrophe. But, if we fail to hear God's warnings, whether in regard to economic justice, climate change, or democracy, catastrophe is likely to occur,

---

1   Abraham Joshua Heschel, *The Prophets* (Peabody, MA: Hendrickson, 1962), volume 2, 3-4.
2   Ibid., vol. 1, 14.
3   Ibid, vol. 2, 11.

either through acts of nature, internal strife, or external threat. Similar to process theology, Heschel describes the prophetic challenge to listen to "the voice that God has lent to the silent agony, a voice to the plundered poor, to the profaned riches of the world."[4]

Biblical scholar Walter Brueggemann asserts that prophetic faith involves "direct, confrontational encounter with established power," whether religious, economic, or political.[5] For Brueggemann, "The task of prophetic ministry is to nurture, nourish, and evoke a consciousness and perception alternative to the consciousness and perception of the dominant culture around us."[6] The prophet proclaims a spiritual alternative to the "religion of static triumphalism and the politics of oppression and exploitation."[7] Prophets challenge us to forsake complacency with injustice to experience lament and urgency. We are in real trouble: the writing is on the wall in terms of social upheaval, economic inequality, racism and heterosexism, and climate denial. The future of our nation and planet are at risk, and we are close to, or have already passed, the point of no return. Prophetic critique begins with "the capacity to grieve because that is the most visceral announcement that things are not right."[8] Denial, numbness, and apathy must give way to regret, confession, and repentance. Opening to our grief and despair may inspire actions that will save us from the consequences of our previous denial. Confession and lamentation are the foundation of national healing, and the inspiration to personal and political transformation.

Prophets imaginatively see the world as it could be if the powerful and privileged sacrificed for the greater good – blue skies and clean water, celebration on tribal lands, children achieving their full potential, and families delighting in safe and comfortable shelter, education, and nutrition. A world in which African American parents no longer have to give the "talk" to their preteen and teenage boys. All this is possible, the prophet believes, but it requires

---

4   Ibid., vol, 1, 5.
5   Walter Brueggemann, *The Prophetic Imagination* (Minneapolis: Fortress Press, 2001), ix.
6   Ibid., 3.
7   Ibid., 5.
8   Ibid., 11.

a great imaginative leap based on the willingness of the powerful and privileged to lament and sacrifice and move from self-interest to human heartedness and earth care. The privileged, even if they see themselves as morally upright, must face the facts, and their own complicity, in America's history of racism, genocide, sexism, and homophobia. As individuals and citizens, we must live more simply and advocate for social, political, and economic transformation so others may simply live.

German theologian and activist Dorothee Soelle announces that "We're all mystics! That sentence contains in itself the right of every human being to beauty and vision." Then she asks, "Is there such a thing as a human right to behold God?" According to Soelle, "mysticism is the experience of the oneness and wholeness of life," and the contrasting "unrelenting perception of how fragmented life is," as a result of injustice and violence. "Finding God fragmented into the rich and poor, top and bottom, sick and well, weak and mighty: that's the mystic's suffering" which leads to prophetic resistance against the unjust and destructive status quo, fostered by governments, institutions, and personal abuse. Life is intended to be beautiful. Indeed, the teleology of the universe is aimed at the production of beauty," according to Whitehead. "The resistance of St. Francis or Elizabeth of Thuringia or Martin Luther King grew out of the perception of beauty. And the long-lasting and most dangerous resistance is the one that is born from beauty."[9]

Soelle denies "the distinction between a mystical *internal and a political external.*"[10] She asserts that "there is no experience of God that can be so privatized that it becomes and remains the property of one owner, the privilege of a person of leisure, the esoteric domain of the initiated."[11] Soelle believes that we need to join "both the inner light of being one with every living thing, and the resistance against the machine of death,"[12] Then and now, prophetic experience and process theology begins with the encounter

9   Dorothee Soelle, *The Silent Cry: Mysticism and Resistance,* (Minneapolis: Fortress Press, 2001), 302.
10 Ibid., 3.
11 Ibid., 3.
12 Ibid., 5.

with God and then expands to claim the whole earth as the object of God's quest for Shalom and our vocation as God's agents in world healing.

PROPHETIC PROCESS

Process theology is profoundly holistic and embodied in spirit. While we need the God-like vision of the prophets, we must join this transcendent vision with God's down-to-earth spiritual, ethical, and institutional practices. Prophetic spirituality and politics join the God's-eye view with confrontation with the forces of injustice and violence to heal the soul of the nation and protect the future of the planet. Accordingly, each chapter will conclude with a prophetic process practice to energize our commitment to healing the world.

Prophetic faith is grounded in empathy. We experience the cries of the poor, and so does God. God is the "fellow sufferer," who understands, and who awakens us to the relationship between our pain and the pain of the world. Prophetic faith opens us to feeling the cost of injustice for the oppressed and oppressor alike. While the oppressed may lose their lives, the oppressor may gain the world and lose their soul. In the dynamic interdependence of life, described by process theology, we create one another in our relationships, social context, and history. "I am because of you, we are because of one another," *ubuntu.*

One of my spiritual mentors is the African-American mystic, Howard Thurman, the contemplative leader of the American civil rights movement. His work *Jesus and the Disinherited,* perhaps the first African-American liberation theology, inspired Martin Luther King. King carried Thurman's book in his satchel during the heart of the civil rights protests.

One autumn, young Howard worked for a white store owner, raking leaves. After he raked them in a pile, the store owner's preschool daughter decided to play a game. Whenever she saw a brightly colored leaf, she scattered the whole pile to show it to Howard. She did this several times until Howard told her to stop. When she failed to heed Howard's warning, he threatened to tell her father. Angry at his rebuke, the young girl jabbed him with a straight pen. When he cried out, the girl responded, "O Howard, that didn't hurt you. You can't feel."[13] She had inherited the racist viewpoint that African Americans are different in kind than white Americans, and that, like animals, they cannot feel the pain we inflict on them. In contrast, process theologians believe the universe is a theatre for feeling, and that the non-human world is a locus of experience and accordingly deserves ethical consideration.

In this practice, take time to be still, breathing deeply your connection with the world around you and feeling the calm that comes from being still and knowing that God is with you. (Psalm 46:10) In quiet, ask God to give you an empathetic spirit. Ask God to awaken your senses to the cries of the poor and the hopelessness of the marginalized. In the quiet, as you experience your connection with the world around you, let images of our world fill your consciousness.

Today, as I pondered our deep spiritual connectedness, I saw images of people worried about clean drinking water in Flint, Michigan, and East Palestine, Ohio;[14] children fleeing violence in Central America; families experiencing bombing Ukraine; refugees and displaced persons in Palestine, Somalia, and Afghanistan; parents and family members grieving the loss of children due to school shootings and police violence; and the cries of non-human animals, at risk through climate change. I also felt my anger at politicians and media personalities fomenting violence and national division in the United States through prevarication and incivility; business leaders and politicians putting gun ownership and profit above the lives of children; and global leaders threatening nuclear war.

Take these feelings to God in prayer. Ask God to give you a spiritual restlessness, joined with a deep peace, to inspire you to change what you cannot accept and to respond personally and politically to injustice and claim your vocation as God's companion in healing the earth.

---

13 Howard Thurman, *With Heart and Mind* (New York: Harcourt Brace and Company, 1979), 12.
14 On February 3, 2023, a train, operated by Norfolk Southern, carrying chemicals and combustible materials, with vinyl chloride, a toxic flammable gas, derailed, releasing toxins in the air and water supply.

CHAPTER TWO

PROPHETIC PROCESS THEOLOGY

The worship of God is not a rule of safety
— it is an adventure of spirit, the flight after the
unattainable. The death of religion comes with
the repression of the high hope of adventure.[15]

Prophets are spiritual, ethical, and political adventurers. Worshipping God through prophetic activism, joining inner experience and outer transformation, is often dangerous to both the status quo and the prophet. Prophets are regularly objects of suspicion, hatred, and even martyrdom. Their encounters with God propel them onto the high seas of political and spiritual adventure, where prophets seldom find safety, and receive few guarantees of success, but ultimately experience the peace that comes from letting go, as Whitehead says, of the self-interest of isolated individualism to embrace the great Self of companionship with God.

I believe that life-changing theology and spirituality involves the interplay of vision, promise, and practice: visionary experiences of God which give birth to theological world views; the promise that others can experience our world view and mystic vision; and practices that facilitate our experiences of the Holy and its ethical and political demands. Prophetic spirituality begins with a vision of God, conveyed in images, intuitions, words, and insights. Isaiah encounters God in the Jerusalem Temple and is overwhelmed by angelic praises proclaiming, "…the whole earth is full of God's glory." He is promised wholeness and transformation, and then hears God's call, "whom shall we send?" (Isaiah 6:1-8). The word of God comes to Amos, setting him on a journey from his comfortable life in Judah to proclaim God's call to justice to the Northern Kingdom. He receives divine intuitions and visionary experiences describing the Northern Kingdom's future; calls for repentance, grounded in economic and social justice; and is given God's prom-

---

15 Alfred North Whitehead, *Science and the Modern World* (New York: Free Press, 1997), 192.

ise that beyond national tragedy, new life will emerge. Both Amos and Isaiah join spirituality and ethics, and mysticism and political protest. They feel the currents of God's moral and spiritual arcs and convey the contours of God's challenge to a wayward people.

Today, process theology charts a similar prophetic course: it portrays a vision of God which we can experience first-hand when we allow ourselves to be transformed by spiritual practices and ethical and political behaviors. The heartbeat of prophetic process theology includes the following theological affirmations, grounded in experience, generalized on the mountaintop of reflection, and embodied in the day-to-day quest for solidarity with God, the ultimate Empath, Visionary, and Change Agent.

1) *The Process is the Reality.* Life is an ever-flowing stream, coursing through our cells and souls. Life is constantly moving forward even in times when the moral arc of history appears to be blocked by wayward and recalcitrant leaders. We can't go back to a historical or national golden age, when people knew their place in society, didn't rock the boat, and respected the authority of their betters. We can't deny the achievements and errors of the past. Whether or not we admit it, we must let new visions emerge. We must welcome new ways of looking at our history, whether articulated by critical race theory, the science of sexuality, or studies of global climate change. The pure conservative, looking back at a golden age and seeking to return to the glory days of 1950s America, when diversity was in the closet and separate but equal was acceptable to persons of faith, is going against the nature of the universe and its Adventurous God. Glory Hallelujah! God's truth is marching on! "Let justice roll down like water and righteousness like an ever-flowing stream" (Amos 5:24).

2) *Relationship is Everything.* We are persons of history, birthed from our environment and then called to shape the world that brought us forth. The whole universe conspires to create each moment of experience and in this moment of experience, we have the freedom to become agents of our destiny, personal and political. Process theology advocates an ethics of *ubuntu*, "I am because of you. We are because of one another." In the spirit of process theology, Martin Luther King proclaims:

10

> It all boils down to this, that all life is interrelated. We
> are caught in an inescapable network of mutuality, tied into
> a single garment of destiny. Whatever affects one directly,
> affects all indirectly. We are made to live together because of
> the interrelated structure of reality.[16]

Our global communications testify to the interdependence of life. My experience is profoundly shaped by images from the morning news as well as conversations about local newsfeeds with my wife over the breakfast table. Empathy is built into the nature of reality, despite our attempts to deny it. Spiritual and community health are achieved when we embrace our connectedness with life around us, our personal and historical past, and the Intimate God who moves lovingly and creatively to redeem the past, inspire the present, and give hope for the future. Today, more than ever, we must affirm the words of Martin Luther King, "We have made the world a neighborhood, and yet we have not had the ethical commitment to make it a brotherhood."[17] The call of relationship is toward the Beloved Community, the community of empathy and adventure, in which our joys and sorrows are one, in which the healing of persons leads to a healed social order and a healed social order promotes the healing of persons.

3) *Democracy of the Spirit.* Process theology affirms the universality of experience and value. The universe is alive. While levels of experience vary in intensity, sensitivity, and stature, every creature experiences the universe from its perspective. This is the meaning of pan-experientialism. While rocks don't have centered selves as we do most of the time, the molecules and particles that compose a rock respond to their environment, albeit in simple ways. Plants, trees, ants, and bees interact with the world around them in ways that suggest the presence of an inner spirit or intelligence.

Rights and responsibilities depend on the ultimacy and ubiquity of experience, and the energy of experience that unites all life forms. When the merchant's daughter exclaims "you can't feel"

16 Martin Luther King, *Testament of Hope* (New York: HarperOne, 2003), 254.

17 Martin Luther King, edited by Clayborne Carson and Peter Holloran, *A Knock at Midnight* (New York: Warner Books, 1978), 201.

to Howard Thurman, she is implicitly exempting him from the experience that is associated with white persons (full-fledged humans!!!) like herself and her family. Viewed as unable to feel the way "higher organisms" do, persons of color were judged as being part of a different order than their white companions and accordingly neither needed nor deserved the same levels of education, ethical consideration, and accessibility to democracy.

The democracy of spirit affirmed by process theology and creation-based mysticism widens the scope of respect and ethical consideration, and challenges us to embrace what mystic-physician-theologian Albert Schweitzer called "reverence for life." While life is robbery, as Whitehead observes, and creatures are often at cross purposes as prey and predator, our destruction of other life forms requires moral justification. Process theology affirms the wisdom of the Psalmist who described a world of praise:

> Praise the LORD from the earth,
>> you sea monsters and all deeps,
>>> fire and hail, snow and frost,
>>> stormy wind fulfilling his command!
>> Mountains and all hills,
>>> fruit trees and all cedars!
>> Wild animals and all cattle,
>>> creeping things and flying birds!
>> Kings of the earth and all peoples,
>>> princes and all rulers of the earth!
>>> Young men and women alike,
>>> old and young together! (Psalm 150:7-10)

Panexperientialism recognizes the organic unity of life and goes beyond dualities that separate humankind from the non-human world, our animal companions, and our fellow humans. We can oppose a political or business leader's decisions vehemently and still view them as God's beloved children, whose injustice harms them as well as those they manipulate, marginalize, and oppress. We can all "feel." There is no "other." We are joined in an intricate and interdependent tapestry of experience and relatedness.

4) *Image of God.* The biblical tradition speaks of humankind, male and female, created in image of a wise, creative, and loving God. While process theology affirms God's loving presence in all life forms, not just human, and challenges us to world loyalty and reverence for life, process theology also recognizes the unique giftedness of humankind. We are, like God, history makers, creators, and lovers. Immersed in the non-human world, our complexity of experience enables us to soar into the heavens, delight in imagination, sacrifice for a greater good, and challenge ourselves to grow spiritually and relationally. The image of God in humankind in all its cultural, intellectual, religious, and sexual diversity, inspires those who follow the better angels of their nature to see holiness in every person, and aim at equal rights, justice, economic opportunity, and freedom of expression for all. The image of God motivates the prophets' challenge to any practice that defaces human value and prevents humans from living abundantly and fully. The image of God demands equality of opportunity, regardless of gender, race, nation of origin, age, or any other of the varieties of human identity.

5) *Partnership with God.* Prophetic spirituality affirms the creativity and agency of all persons. While we are shaped by our environment, family of origin, and inherited belief systems, we can break free of the limitations of the past. We can see differently and live differently. The biblical prophets affirmed the importance of freedom, the freedom to repent and change our minds and lifestyles, to go beyond prejudice and nationalism, and to live lovingly and globally. "Perhaps," the prophet Amos avers, the wealthy and powerful will seek justice, and "perhaps," God will change God's mind and provide the resources for national survival. The future is open, whether in terms of our individual lives or national priorities. We are, along with God, world shapers who can choose either life or death for ourselves and the world. Created in the image of God, our vocation is to be God's companions in healing the world. God cannot heal the world without us. The moral and spiritual arcs require our cooperation and commitment to fully shape the historical process. We matter to God and we matter to one another.

6) *Divine Restlessness.* Process theology affirms that God is catalyst for growth and change.

In every situation, God's aim is the best for the impasse, the highest possibility available given our previous values and past history. God has a vision and implants the divine vision of Shalom in human and non-human history. The Deep Peace of God is balanced by the Holy Restlessness of the Spirit, which judges every person and nation in terms of what it can become in God's Realm of Shalom.

Process theology sees God's power as defined by love. The inspiration for change, growth, justice, and equality, God acts lovingly and persuasively, and does not dominate or dictate. God's presence in the universe motivates inspires the power of love, not the love of power. Authoritarian, unilateral, domineering, and dualistic images of God inspire dualistic, divisive, domineering, and destructive uses of power. The divine right of kings, the subjugation of women, indigenous peoples, and political opponents, finds its model in images of God as unbending, legalistic, all-controlling, and punitive in nature. Divine absolutism leads to political absolutism and division of the world into friend and foe and us and them. The dualistic and authoritarian divine potentate tells us that while we may recognize, for example, that immigrants and asylum seekers share our humanity, they do not share our human rights, thus allowing us to separate toddlers from their parents, and define immigrants as thugs and rapists. In contrast, the relational image of God championed by process theology encourages democratic decision-making, religious and ethnic diversity and pluralism, affirmation of the varieties of sexual identity, political and ideological civility, and hospitality toward strangers, immigrants, and asylum seekers. God has poured God's Spirit on all flesh and calls all flesh its wondrous diversity toward wholeness and love. God challenges everything that stands in the way of our full humanity and inspires us to be God's partners in the process of interpersonal, economic, and political restoration and healing.

7) *Empathetic God.* Alfred North Whitehead describes God as "the fellow sufferer who understands."[18] God is also the great

18 Alfred North Whitehead, *Process and Reality: Corrected Edition,* (New York: Free Press, 1979), 351.

companion who celebrates. In the spirit of the Hebraic prophets, the God of process theology takes note of and is shaped by what happens in the world. The God of the Hebraic prophets mourned farm foreclosures and the reality of widows (a term to describe the powerless and marginalized) unable to feed their children. God also felt anger at religious rituals and celebrations that drowned out the cries of the poor. Worship without justice is an affront to the Great Empath:

> I hate, I despise your festivals,
> and I take no delight in your solemn assemblies.
> Even though you offer me your burnt offerings and grain offerings,
> I will not accept them…
> Take away from me the noise of your songs;
> I will not listen to the melody of your harps.
> But let justice roll down like water
> and righteousness like an ever-flowing stream.
> (Amos 5:21-24)

The Great Empath is also the Great Democrat and Ultimate Relativist who hears the cries of the poor and confronts the machinations of the powerful and wealthy, seeks equality of humankind while treating each person uniquely. God does not seek equality of outcome, for our destinations are as unique as our personalities, gifts, and life histories. Rather, in the spirit of I Corinthians 12, God dispenses divine blessings abundantly and intimately, and promotes the creation of communities in which the gifts of all people can be expressed for the wellbeing of the whole.

> Now there are varieties of gifts but the same Spirit, and there are varieties of services but the same Lord, and there are varieties of activities, but it is the same God who activates all of them in everyone. To each is given the manifestation of the Spirit for the common good (1 Corinthians 12:4-7).

Each gift matters within the Body of Christ, the Beloved Community, in which everyone is inspired, treasured, and affirmed. God delights in a child playing soccer and writing a story. God shouts "hallelujah" when an adult claims a neglected talent in retirement. God raises God's voice with those who protest. When we express our giftedness in response to the world's needs, we can, as runner and later missionary Eric Liddell, portrayed in "Chariots of Fire," affirms, "feel God's pleasure." The Creative Wisdom of the Universe aims at beauty in the evolution of galaxies, the growth of communities, and the spiritual maturation of persons. The prophet challenges the powerful to "do something beautiful for God" in creating healthy workplaces, providing fair salaries, promoting educational opportunities, and awakening citizenship. The prophet energizes persons at the margins to claim their voice, discover their value and giftedness, and work for the fullest expression of all people in a truly healthy and life-affirming social order.

Prophetic Process

One of my spiritual mentors Allan Armstrong Hunter, a companion of Howard Thurman in the Fellowship of Reconciliation, penned a poem to describe the spirit of the contemplative prophet. Hunter counsels, "we can all breathe our own versions of a prayer which my wife and I developed through the years (perhaps thinking each first line while inhaling and each second line while exhaling)." In the spirit of the Hunters, awaken to God breathing through, empowering you like the frightened disciples to go out into the world as God's healing and justice-seeking companions.

I breathe your blue sky deeply in
To blow it gladly back again!
I breathe your shining beauty in
To call forth the buried talent in me.
I breathe your healing energy in
To vibrate through each body cell.
We breathe your reconciling spirit in
To bring peace in us, and in the world.
We breathe your resurrection power in
To make our relationships new and glad.

We breathe your strength and warmth and humor in
To share joyously with all we meet.[19]

You may take this prayer with you as you walk, in meetings, as a prelude to watching the news or during commercials, in greeting a child or companion, to center your spirit and enable you to find guidance to bring beauty to every encounter and swim gracefully in synch with God's ever-flowing streams of justice.

19 Quoted in Harvey Seifert, *Explorations in Meditation and Contemplation* (Nashville: Upper Room, 1981), 10.

CHAPTER THREE

PROPHETIC MYSTICISM

This is what the Lord GOD showed me: he
was forming locusts at the time the latter growth
began to sprout (it was the latter growth after the
king's mowings). When they had finished eating
the grass of the land, I said,

"O Lord God, forgive, I beg you!
How can Jacob stand?
He is so small!"
The LORD relented concerning this;
"It shall not be," said the Lord. (Amos 7:1-3)

Process mystics are visionaries, who walk with God and talk with God. The word of God intuitively and inspirationally comes to Amos. The farmer and shepherd knows that he must leave the comfort of home to speak a word of challenge and condemnation to his northern kin. He receives verbal guidance and a vision of what might happen if the people don't change their way. Amos contends with the God who calls him, begging for mercy for the Northern Kingdom, and his pleas open up new possibilities for divine action. God changes God's mind!

Isaiah unexpectedly encounters the living God, while seeking a moment of peace, during a time of national instability. He catches a vision of God on the divine throne, the center of creation, the heart of the people, and glimpses a glory-filled world, and then confronted by the call to becomes God's emissary to a wayward nation.

Mary of Nazareth says "yes" to God's incarnational invitation and is inspired to speak for the poor and dispossessed and proclaim a new world order, the age of Shalom.

He has brought down the powerful from their thrones
and lifted up the lowly;

he has filled the hungry with good things
and sent the rich away empty.
He has come to the aid of his child Israel,
in remembrance of his mercy,
according to the promise he made to our ancestors,
to Abraham and to his descendants forever. (Luke 1:52-55)

Thirty years later, her son Jesus, baptized by John in the Jordan River and identified by Spirit as God's chosen messenger, God's Beloved Son, proclaims "The time is fulfilled, and the kingdom of God has come near; repent, and believe in the good news" (Mark 1:15) and claims his spiritual mission as God's anointed:

to bring good news to the poor....
to proclaim release to the captives
and recovery of sight to the blind,
to set free those who are oppressed,
to proclaim the year of the Lord's favor. (Luke 4:18-19)

Filled with the same world-changing spirit as his mother, Jesus proclaims that the Jubilee year has arrived. Shalom is in our midst. The prophetic voice, inspired by God, speaks a word for this time and all times.

Prophetic Mystics. The power and message of the prophetic comes from the prophet's encounter with God. God is alive, the prophet's heartbeat and inspiration, and the words of the prophet's mouth will give glory to God and challenge to the world, regardless of the consequences to the prophet and his community. The prophet sees the Infinite in the finite, and the Eternal in the concrete, embodying God's moral and spiritual arc in the challenges and conflicts of history.

In the first volume of this trilogy, *Process Theology and Mysticism,* I described an affirmative, socially active, and prophetic mysticism. Encountering God widens the scope of our compassion and awakens us to our deepest selves as well as the well-being of the planet. From the perspective of process theology, the mystical path is prophetic and inspires us to embrace God's aim at healing and wholeness. The movement of prophetic mysticism embraces the following non-linear steps, involving the dynamic interplay of awakening, affirming, simplifying, expanding, and transforming.

1) *Awakening to God's grandeur illuminating all creation and every human being.* Mystics are spiritually "woke." Prophetic mystics experience God's light shining in every person and all creation. The heavens declare the glory of God and every person reveals the face of God. To see the light is to share the light and this means challenging injustice and creating structures that promote human and planetary healing and justice.

2) *Affirming the Universe as a Reflection of God's Movements in Body, Mind, and Spirit.* Prophetic process theology is characterized by world-affirmation. God loves our cells as well as our souls. God loves the friend and stranger and invites us to embrace the joys and sorrows of our world. Recognizing the distance between the moral character of our world and God's vision of Shalom creates a spiritual restlessness that takes us beyond duality to unity with all creation.

3) *Simplifying Our Focus and Decluttering Our Spirit.* Traditionally identified with the path of purgation, the prophetic mystic commits to spiritual and material simplicity. In the spirit of Jesus' words from John 15, prophetic mysticism prunes away everything that stands between us and God. Grounded in practicing the presence of God in every encounter and decision, the quest for simplicity opens us to experiencing God's moment- by-moment and long-term vision in our lives and in the world around us. Simplicity of life joins us with creation and with those who lack life's basics. By practicing simplicity, we become good stewards of our economies and ecologies. We live simply so others might simply live.

4) *Expanding Our Compassion and Empathy.* In the words of St. Bonaventure and Nicholas of Cusa, God is a circle or infinite sphere whose "center is everywhere and whose circumference is nowhere." Prophetic faith begins with the personal faith of the prophet. Prophetic ministry requires self-affirmation and self-care. Recognizing the inner light of God within us, we expand the circle of affirmation to include all creation. We learn, as Jesus of Naza-

reth counseled, to love our neighbor as ourselves. Discovering that there is no "other," we see our neighbor's joy as contributory to our own fulfillment. The quality of our lives is enhanced by our compassionate care. We want everyone to have an opportunity for abundant life. Just as injustice and incivility harm the souls of those who perpetrate alienation and superiority, commitment to justice, restoration, and equality expands our souls and energizes our spirits.

5) *Transforming Ourselves and Our World.* Prophetic faith imagines a new heaven and a new earth and creates infrastructures for initiating and expanding God's realm on earth as it is in heaven. Creative transformation may involve deconstruction, and breaking down everything that stands in the way of justice and healing, and this applies to the prophet as well as their people. The process is the reality, and the reality involves a commitment to constant growth and change. We can never be content with the world as it is when the world that could become calls us forward. As the Apostle Paul challenges, "Do not be conformed to this world, but be transformed by the renewing of your minds, so that you may discern what is the will of God - what is good and acceptable and perfect" (Romans 12:2). The will of God reflects God's vision of Shalom, incarnate in our lives and the world. Still, the goal of all prophetic protest and deconstruction is healing and restoration, reparation and uniting.

We are all mystics, Dorothee Soelle reminds us. We are all also prophets in the making if we listen to the voice of God calling us from waywardness to mindfulness, self-interest to compassion, and isolated individualism to world loyalty.

PROPHETIC PROCESS

Process theology describes a God-filled universe. God is our deepest reality. Spiritual practices enable us to bring God's vision to light, to make the ever-present God fully present in our daily lives. Process theology takes us beyond the dualities of light and darkness, friend and foe, fellow citizen and immigrant, and human and non-human. The true light of God enlightens us and all creation. In Jesus' ethical-prophetic manifesto, the Sermon on the Mount, Jesus proclaimed to his followers:

> *You are the light of the world. A city built*
> *on a hill cannot be hid. People do not light a*
> *lamp and put it under the bushel basket; rather,*
> *they put it on the lamp stand, and it gives light*
> *to all in the house. In the same way, let your light*
> *shine before others, so that they may see your good*
> *works and give glory to your Father in heaven.*
> (Matthew 5:14-16)

Finding our light. Enabling us to see the light within illuminates our lives and is a crucial step toward the self-care and self-affirmation necessary to sustain prophetic protest. It also brings light to the world. Our spiritual growth is our gift to the world, giving glory to God by bringing beauty to the world and excising every impediment to the global experience of God's abundant life.

In this prophetic exercise, begin with quiet prayer. Ask God to help you see the light in yourself and others. Ask God to heal everything that stands in the way of your experiencing of your divine identity.

Breathe slowly and deeply God's light. Let it fill you, surround you, and radiate from you. Now let your breath radiate into the world. Visualize your breath radiating out into the world, embracing in larger and larger circles your family, community, nation, and the planet. Visualize your light surrounding the leaders of your nation, the leaders of nations with whom your nation is alienated, and politicians and business leaders whose policies you detest. They too are God's children, and in need of healing.

In the days ahead, take time to pray that God will show you places where you need to bring God's light to the world and then let your light shine.

CHAPTER FOUR

PROPHETIC CHALLENGE

God confronts the actual with what is
possible for it...Every act leaves the world with
a deeper or fainter impress of God. He then
passes in his next relationship to the world with
enlarged, or diminished, presentation of ideal
values.[20]

Reflecting the presence of the Infinite in the finite, prophetic faith is profoundly historical and concrete. The prophet identifies dishonest political and business leaders and describes injustice. The prophet's God is embedded in history. God has a stake in the survival of the planet, in healthy governance, school board decisions, and the price of milk and eggs. While morality and politics are guided by theological truths pertaining to life as a totality, these truths find their meaning in application to flesh and blood situations. When Jesus asserts "as you did it to one of the least of these brothers and sisters of mine, you did it to me," he is pointing to concrete people and situations then and now (Matthew 25:40). His eye on the sparrow, and also on the homeless family unable to get governmental assistance, the gay son disowned by his parents, the grieving sister whose brother is the victim of the mass school shooting in Uvalde, Texas, the transgendered teen bullied at school, and the senior adult who must choose between medications and groceries.

Affirming the "teleology of the universe is toward the production of beauty," inspires us with gratitude and wonder. But, without action, embodied in doing something beautiful for God – deepening God's impress on the world – our cosmic appreciation is incomplete. The prophet challenges leaders to create structures of love, compassion, beauty, and justice. "Liberty and justice for all" – not some – demands denouncing the widening gap between the rich and poor, furthered by unequal tax policies and passing down of wealth; protesting police violence against persons of col-

---

20 Whitehead, *Religion in the Making*, 153, 152.

or; strict laws related to gun ownership; and electing officials who trust science whether it relates to vaccines, education, or climate change. Prophets recognize that the social nature of life gives institutions, businesses, and governments the power to support or destroy millions of persons.

Individual action is essential in the interdependence of life. The world is saved one action at a time. Individual hospitality and generosity are not sufficient to transform unjust and death-dealing institutions. We must feed the hungry; we must also ensure that every child across the globe is fed, and that requires a transformation of our vocation as citizens and the creation of systems of hospitality, compassion, and justice.

In this chapter, I will address three seemingly intractable issues from a process prophetic perspective – climate change, racial and ethnic divisiveness, and economic injustice - recognizing that there are many paths to achieving the Beloved and Just Community. While the scope of my analysis and response is brief, I hope that it inspires your own prophetic research and involvement.

While prophets then and now recognize the dire nature of the problems we face and our failure to respond, they also believe that when we partner with God to heal the world, unexpected energies of creativity and healing emerge that contribute to healing the soul of the nation and planet. Realistic about our situation, the prophet recognizes the great "perhaps" of divine-human partnership in renewing the earth and our political institutions.

Confronting Climate Change. Thursday, February 23, 2023, the day after Ash Wednesday, temperatures in our Washington D.C. suburb reached nearly 80 degrees Fahrenheit, one of the highest recorded temperatures in the past seventy-five years. Although I joyfully donned my shorts and a T-shirt for my afternoon walk, I also felt uneasy. Eighty degrees in winter! Is this a portent for what is to come this summer and in the years to come? That same day, there were blizzards an hour north of Los Angeles! As one meteorologist noted, "weather is mood, climate is personality." By all accounts, the personality of the planet is changing rapidly. Climate change is threatening human and non-human life, destroying habitats, melting glaciers and icebergs, and causing extreme weather patterns.

The environmental crisis cries out for prophetic voices. In 1971, process theologian John Cobb asked, "Is it too late?" to respond to the environmental crisis. Five decades later, the echoes of the Hebraic prophets resound in teenage Greta Thunberg's voice to the world's leaders:

> You have stolen my dreams and my childhood with
> your empty words… People are suffering. People are dying.
> Entire ecosystems are collapsing. We are in the beginning of
> a mass extinction, and all you can talk about is money and
> fairy tales of eternal economic growth. How dare you![21]

For those who have eyes to see and ears to hear, the reality of global climate change is clear.[22] The burning of fossil fuels has resulted in global temperature rise, warming oceans, shrinking ice sheets, glacial retreat, decreased snow cover, accelerating sea level rise, declining Arctic Sea ice, extreme weather events, and ocean acidification is transforming our world, creating wastelands where there were once woodlands and putting at risk human and non-human habitats. Forests are burning and coral reefs are dying. Two-thirds of bird species in North America are at risk of extinction. An insect apocalypse is on the horizon. Rachel Carson's vision of a "silent spring" may be the future that awaits our children and grandchildren. Climate change, and the extinction of flora and fauna, have contributed to drought, political instability, and immigration. "What's at stake here is a livable world," warns Robert Watson, chair of the Intergovernmental Science-Policy Platform on Biodiversity and Ecosystem Services.[23]

---

21 Transcript: Greta Thunberg's Speech at the U.N. Climate Action Summit, NPR, September 23, 2019, https://www.npr.org/2019/09/23/763452863/transcript-greta-thunbergs-speech-at-the-u-n-climate-action-summit (accessed September 3, 2022).

22 I am grateful for the analysis of our current environmental crisis, penned by my student Allen Ewing-Merrill in his D.Min. thesis, "Vocation, Formation, Imagination, and Transformation: Spiritual Leadership for a Climate-Changed World."

23 Elizabeth Kolbert, "Climate Change and the New Age of Extinction," *The New Yorker, May 20, 2019.* https://www.newyorker.com/magazine/2019/05/20/climate-change-and-the-new-age-of-extinction

United Church of Christ pastor and ecological activist Jim Antal calls our situation a "theological emergency." Antal believes that "God is calling the church to speak with a clear, bold, truthful, and prophetic voice in a time of climate crisis."[24] This may be, as environmentalist Bill McKibben asserts, "...an opportunity for which the church was born."[25]

The non-dual and relational vision of process theology provides a theological and spiritual foundation for ecological conversion. We are part of nature, intimately connected to the non-human world. What happens to the seas and skies happens to us. What we do cures or kills creation around us. Embedded in nature, our vocation is to be gardeners and protectors of non-human life. The world is alive at every level. Non-human life is valuable and beloved by God. What happens to creation happens to God. Our choices shape what God can do. God laments, and calls us to lament, the death of species and threats to future generations. God feels the panic of a polar bear drowning in the Arctic. God experiences the loss of beauty that accompanies the death of species of flora and fauna. The One who Loved the World invites us to love the world enough to challenge our leaders to radical change and challenge ourselves to personal simplicity and ecological protest. Awakening to the Divine Imagination, we need to imagine new forms of energy, new dietary habits, transformed communities and transportation systems, and ways to feed and welcome climate refugees. "Perhaps," it is not too late. God cannot save us apart from our companionship: there is no predetermined "second coming" or assured victory over the forces of destruction. God needs our commitment and political action to deepen and energize God's healing presence in the world. God's grace inspires and challenges us. But, without us, God cannot heal the world Jesus came to save and transform.

Healing the Racial Divide. The USA is a fractured nation, and this fragmentation is going global. In North America, anti-Semitism is on the rise. This morning, my newsfeed reported nine anti-Semitic incidents in the Montgomery County, Maryland, public schools, shocking persons like me who find it difficult to

24 Jim Antal, *Climate Church, Climate World,* 52.
25 Jim Antal, *Climate Church, Climate World,* 126.

believe that such acts would occur in our affluent and liberal section of Maryland.[26] Hate crimes against LGBTQ+ persons are on the rise, fomented in part by the rhetoric of reckless politicians, serving "red meat" to culture wars enthusiasts. White nationalism, much of it Christian, is considered the most serious internal terrorist threat by the FBI.

Later in the morning, I was further troubled when a friend posted the occurrence of racist symbolism in Orange County, California.[27] The next day, February 25, a bill was introduced in the Texas assembly to ban legal Chinese persons from purchasing property! Tragically, conservative Christian churches are superspreaders of hatred. The marriage of nationalism, racism, sexism, biblical literalism, and Trumpism is toxic to the United States and to Christianity.

Seeking to pander to racial fears, politicians target American history textbooks and the teaching of Critical Race Theory. Denial of USA history goes along with the re-emergence of the Ku Klux Klan and voter suppression, mostly affecting persons of color, senior adults, and lower income persons. Drag queens, transgender persons, and higher education have become targets as the civil fabric of society threatens to unravel. Political leaders have abandoned the better angels of our nature, fanned the flames of racial, ethnic, and sexual incivility and violence while neglecting poverty, immigration, education, and climate. Police violence directed gratuitously toward persons of color has provoked the affirmations, "Black Lives Matter" and "Say Her/His/Their Name." The better angels of our nature have been abandoned, trumped by fear, hate, exclusion, and parochialism. Does prophetic process theology have a word to say to the divisiveness that privileges those in power, manipulates uneducated whites, and denies diversity and pluralism?

Process theology needs to be prophetic toward itself as well as the nation. At a recent conference celebrating the Fiftieth Anniversary of the Center for Process Theology, there were only a

---

26 Maryland school district aims to stop wave of anti-Semitism (shorenewsnetwork.com), published February 23, 2022.

27 Video: Black students receive racist drawings at California elementary school | CNN, published February 24.

handful of persons of color in a group numbering approximately two hundred. Process theology has often been too elite, too abstract, too male, and too white, and this has blunted our prophetic impact, despite our theological commitment to diversity and pluralism. In the spirit of the Hebraic prophets, we must look at ourselves, critiquing our own values, along with the values of our culture and politics.

Still, despite its fallibility and limitations, process theology can be a resource for prophetic transformation. Process theology affirms, first of all, that God is a political and cultural adventurer, not the protector of the status quo. Whitehead's term "adventures of ideas" applies to politics and economics as well as science and philosophy. Process theology undergirds and embraces the prophetic imagination, articulated by Walter Brueggemann, whose vocation is to "nurture, nourish, and evoke a consciousness and perception alternative to the consciousness and perception of the dominant culture around us,"[28] and to *energize* persons and communities by its promise of positive future toward which the community of faith may move, and to promote an alternative vision which inspires "fervent anticipation of the newness that God has promised and will surely give."[29] Process theology nurtures the prophetic "what if" and "what's next" in the quest for justice. The divine restlessness drives us to imagine and then embody institutional and political transformation to bring liberty, justice, and equality to all.

Second, process theology proclaims the universality of experience and value. The affirmation "you can feel" gives birth to honoring all experience as meaningful. Pain and suffering must not just be noted abstractly but felt, healed, and transformed, and this may involve a type of spiritual and political surgery, grounded in love, to eradicate the sources of injustice.

Third, process theology affirms the value and beauty of diversity. God is the ultimate source of diversity in religion, culture, race, and sexuality. God's wisdom brought forth and continues to bring forth diversity, grounded in the unique gifts of persons and institutions. God does not privilege a particular ethnic, racial,

28 Brueggemann, *The Prophetic Imagination*, 3.
29 Ibid., 3.

gender, or sexual expression. God works toward abundant life and the realization of possibility in every human condition and challenges us to do likewise.

Finally, process theology's vision of relationship and non-duality reminds us that there is no "other." We are ultimately united in our interdependence. Within the body of Christ, we need one another to express fully our personal and communal gifts. *Ubuntu,* "we are because of one another," if one suffers, we all suffer, if one succeeds, we all succeed. A non-dual God feels the joy and pain of the world. Speaking for God, Amos shouts, "I hate, I despise your feasts," unless your worship is accompanied by loving actions. Our lives and our politics are our gifts to God, bringing greater joy or sorrow to God's experience. Will we bring greater joy or pain to God's experience?

Challenging Poverty and Economic Injustice. Poverty is epidemic in the United States. The US Census Bureau estimated that 34 million or 10.5% of Americans can be described as poor. Countering that number, a study by the Institute of Policy Studies, suggests that 40 percent of the USA population (nearly 140 million persons) have trouble making ends meet, families who live month to month and for whom an unplanned car repair or visit to the emergency room can be a financial catastrophe.[30] Both estimates of American poverty are appalling, given the growing wealth gap and the astounding financial gains of the top .1% of Americans. USA tax and economic policy clearly privileges the wealthy over the working or unemployed poor. Despite the disparity of wealth and poverty, many Americans, believe that the wealthy deserve their wealth while the poor are responsible for their poverty, will waste any government subsidies, and must justify the slightest extravagance. The poor aren't lazy. Whether in 8th century BCE Israel or 21st century USA, poverty is hard work and traumatizes parents and children, living on the edge of destitution, and, if they are on governmental assistance, forced to justify every expenditure or source of income. Indeed, the "working poor," hard workers toiling at low salaries make up a significant percentage of the USA population.

---

30 Income Inequality - Inequality.org

Process theology joins the voices of prophets, then and now, to denounce the growing gap between rich and poor, home and farm foreclosures, unemployment, and childhood disease that attends poverty. As a theology of the imagination, process theology is appalled to realize that, as Howard Thurman asserts, one of the first casualties of poverty is a child's imagination. All must be able to engage in the adventures of ideas, all must be able to dream, and then have the opportunity to incarnate their dreams in creative action.

Process theology argues for an environmentally sustainable and just economics in which everyone has a stake. The organic relatedness of life affirms that we are all in the same storm and we need see each other in the same boat. Poverty and injustice harm the bodies and spirits of those who are economically impoverished. Affluence without justice destroys the souls of the wealthy and privileged. Jesus tells the story of a man who builds a great barn only to die the evening it is completed (Luke 12:16-21). The privileged can gain the world and lose their souls as a result of denial and apathy. Process theology calls the privileged and powerful to spiritual stature that sees the well-being of all people as interdependent.

Process theology asserts that deep down all persons "feel" the impact of economic justice and so does God. Great cathedrals and praise bands do violence to God if we neglect the economically distressed. The coming of God is here in the face of a hungry child, the hopelessness of an unemployed parent, and the pain of an asylum seeker, not in some constantly updated faux Second Coming.

As people of stature, we must compassionately embrace every North American and European child. We must also find practical ways to welcome and support climate refugees, asylum seekers, war immigrants, and malnourished persons regardless of nation of origin. The fellow sufferer who understands laments every malnourished and unhoused child. The intimate companion who celebrates rejoices in every act of personal and political generosity which ensures the physical wellbeing and economic security of all God's children.

PROPHETIC PROCESS

Jesus counseled his followers to "ask, seek, and knock" (Matthew 7:7-8). In the social gospel classic, *In His Steps,* Charles Sheldon's "Jesus" asks, "What would Jesus do in today's decision-making?" Mother (Saint) Teresa challenges, "Do something beautiful for God." God's aim is for the "best for that impasse," and in asking, we open to God's highest values.

In this prophetic practice, simply ask God for guidance in the micro and macro. Healthy relationships contribute to healthy countries, and healthy countries contribute to healthy relationships. One act can push forward the moral arc of the universe. Ask, listen, and act, throughout the day, to promote wellbeing in personal and political relationships. Prophetic mindfulness will transform your life, improve relationships, and heal the soul of the nation.

CHAPTER FIVE

PROPHETIC HEALING

The glorification of power has broken more
hearts than it has healed… If the world is to find
God, it must find [God] through love and not
fear. [31]

To exist is to exert power. Every family and government ensures its well-being by a measure of coercion, whether in terms of rules, laws, or penalties. National security involves the potential threat of violence. The question the prophets raise, then and now, is "Will our protests alienate or heal? Will we, if we gain power, adopt the same violent and coercive measures as those we have deposed?" Tragically, many revolutions, intending to improve the plight of impoverished and neglected persons succumb to the same violence and authoritarianism the reactionary elites of a previous generation employed: we need only look at the coercive policies of "Marxist" in name only countries like China, Russia, North Korea, and Venezuela. Revolutionary change may lead to suffering, but the suffering, even of the oppressor, must be minimized. They, too, are children of God. Beloved community will not exist without seeing the holiness in oppressor and oppressed alike.

Prophets pray and protest. Prophets contemplate and agitate. Their goal is healing the soul of the nation, including the nation's economic, environmental, election, and educational policies. This dynamic spirit of spiritual wholeness, characteristic of prophetic process theology, joining contemplation and activism, aims at prophetic healing. Prophetic healing involves our willingness to challenge the injustices of our time while maintaining a spiritual vision of God in ourselves and in those with whom we contend in the political and social arenas. Prophetic healing reflects the profound sense of interdependence in which saint and sinner, and oppressor and oppressed, are ultimately joined in God's Beloved Community. The prophetic healer recognizes that healing must

---

31 Whitehead, *Religion in the Making*, 55.

embrace all of us if it is to be lasting for any of us. This is the Beloved Community of which Martin Luther King speaks and the peaceable realm championed by the prophet Isaiah:

> They shall beat their swords into plowshares
> and their spears into pruning hooks;
> nation shall not lift up sword against nation;
> neither shall they learn war any more. (Isaiah 2:4)

In the transformed world, sought by both process theologian and prophet, old enmities are healed, and diversity gives birth to community.

> The wolf shall live with the lamb;
> the leopard shall lie down with the kid;
> the calf and the lion will feed together,
> and a little child shall lead them.
> The nursing child shall play over the hole of the asp,
> and the weaned child shall put its hand on the adder's den.
> They will not hurt or destroy
> on all my holy mountain,
> for the earth will be full of the knowledge of the LORD
> as the waters cover the sea. (Isaiah 11:6, 8-9)

Prophetic language is blunt. The prophets take no political prisoners as they challenge the powerful and privileged to choose life over death to heal the earth and its peoples. They engage in protests, boycotts, debate, and denunciation. But, they are ultimately inspired by the Realm of Shalom, the Realm of God, which embraces all God's children. They seek to expose the truth – and falsehood – of injustice and oppression. They unclothe the emperor and pronounce judgment on the prevaricator. Here we could learn much from political and civil rights leader, John Lewis, who advised, *"I want to see young people in America feel the spirit of the 1960s and find a way to get in the way. To find a way to get in trouble.* **Good trouble**, *necessary trouble."*

Prophets also recognize that injustice destroys the soul of a nation and the souls of unjust and prevaricating perpetrators. As my father's pastor and social activist Michael-Ray Mathews states, white nationalism harms the souls of white people.

Process prophetic faith aims at wholeness of mind, body, spirit, and community. Beyond the dualities that divide is the deeper unity of God's presence in each person. Obvious or opaque, God speaks to us in every encounter and through every person. With the Celtic theologian and spiritual guide Pelagius, process prophetic faith sees the face of God in every newborn child. The original wholeness of creation and each person shines though, albeit dimly, for those with senses to intuit. Justice must be served. Political and economic pressure must be applied. But this pressure is medicinal and surgical. It aims to excise the branches of injustice, so the divine vine of human and planetary wholeness will flourish.

Prophetic process affirms the inner light, something of God, in all persons, and seeks reconciliation, restoration, and reparation, not punishment and penalty. The wealthy must change their ways. The powerful must share power. Laws must be enacted that compel the wealthy to pay their fair share to upbuild the society and redress wrongs done against persons of color and indigenous people. But, ultimately the goal is healing the soul of the nation and the heart of the people. As John Lewis counsels, *"What I try to tell young people is that if you come together with a mission, and it's grounded with* **love** *and a sense of community, you can make the impossible possible."* Through all the tumult and strife, the prophet is clear about two great things: God is love and God wants us to love one another.

PROPHETIC PROCESS

Beyond duality, there is community. The place of the greatest violence – the Cross – can be the inspiration to love and reconciliation. Even among prophets, there is a temptation to divide and destroy. Each one of us has persons we love to hate, political leaders whom we assume are subhuman, diabolical, and undeserving of our compassion. Yet, it is possible for even those who walk in darkness to see a great light. It is possible for our senses to open and discover that even while we protest, we must see the holiness in perpetrators of injustice. We must open our senses to see the hurt and abused child in a national leader. The fear motivating the gun rights activist. The shriveled souls of those who engage in racism, anti-Semitism, and environmental destruction for the sake of profit or political gain alone. We must picket and pray and challenge and conciliate.

Prophetic mindfulness requires a commitment to self-examination. Unless we are self-aware, we may repeat the injustice and violence of those whose policies and actions we denounce. After a time of prayerful silence, consider the questions: Who am I tempted to hate? Toward whom am I tempted to commit acts of violence? Who do I view as subhuman and worthy of destruction?

In my case, this practice elicited the names of historic evil-doers such as Hitler and members of the Ku Klux Klan. I also discovered my antipathy toward anti-maskers and certain groups denouncing science, whether it relates to vaccination or climate change, white Christian nationalists, and well-known conservative and populist politicians. I recognized that my healing and the healing of my vocation as a prophetic healer depend on loving them despite my protest and opposition.

The next step is to turn to God in prayer. To pray for the healing of your heart and attitudes, and the healing of those you are tempted to hate. Pray that God's will, God's vision for them, will fill their hearts and minds, on God's terms not yours. Pray that they may find peace and wholeness as God's Beloved children.

CHAPTER SIX

PROPHETIC HOPE

At the heart of the nature of things, there
are always the dream of youth and the harvest
of tragedy. The Adventure of the Universe starts
with the dream and reaps Tragic Beauty. This is
the secret of the union of Zest with Peace: - That
the suffering attains its end in a Harmony of
Harmonies. The immediate experience of this
Final Fact, with its union of Youth and Trag-
edy, is the sense of Peace. In this way the world
receives its persuasion toward such perfections as
are possible for its diverse individual occasions.[32]

Over fifty years ago, in what may have been the first theology of ecology, process theology, and my professor and mentor John Cobb asked, "Is it too late?" Even in 1971, Cobb and other environmental pioneers wondered if we had reached the point of no return. Despite the clear evidence that human behaviors shape the environment in significant and often destructive ways, many persons, including powerful business and political leaders, have gone on with our lives as if nothing had changed. The writing is on the wall in terms of climate change, species extinction, earth destruction, racial division, election denying, democracy destruction, and continuing nuclear tensions. The choice is before us – life or death for our nation, future generations, and our planet. Looking at environmental destruction, prophet Greta Thunberg shouts in the spirit of Isaiah and Amos, hoping against hope for a change of heart reflected in changed behaviors:

> For more than thirty years, the science has been crystal clear. How dare you continue to look away and come here saying that you're doing enough, when the politics and solutions needed are still nowhere in sight. You say you hear us and that you understand the urgency. But no matter how sad

---

32 Whitehead, *Religion in the Making*, 55.

and angry I am, I do not want to believe that. Because if you really understood the situation and still kept on failing to act, then you would be evil. And that I refuse to believe.[33]

Like the words of Amos, Hosea, Micah, Jeremiah, and Isaiah, Thunberg is motivated by love. Love of this good earth and love of her parents' and grandparents' generations. Her words echo my experience walking the Capitol Mall in Washington DC, in the 1980s observing hundreds of quilts describing what would be lost if we ever embarked on a planet destroying nuclear war. I wept, and my tears inspired anti-nuclear action. Years later, I walked the Mall, studying the AIDS Quilt, and found a quilt memorializing my high school church friend organist David Keith. My heart was broken and I experienced a healing of homophobia, taking me from uneasiness to affirmation, and alienation to alliance.

Giving up hope is not an option if the soul of the nation and planet are to be healed. But, our hopes must be realistic and concrete and take into consideration that the perils we face as well as process theology's hopeful recognition that within the concrete limitations and perils of life is the inspiration for creative transformation.

Hopelessness takes several forms: denial, emotional powerlessness, apathy, and violence. In denial, we claim there is no problem at all. Everything will work out in the end, or if we don't think about it, it will go away. Emotional powerlessness is the sense of being overwhelmed by the threats, believing we can do nothing about them, and surrendering our agency to powers greater than ourselves. Apathy, often born of ignorance, denies the pain we and others experience, and counsels "eat, drink, and be merry, for tomorrow we will die." Violence separates the world into friend and foe, and seeing no resolution possible, seeks to destroy what we don't understand, is different, or threatens our established values. All these approaches characterize a significant number of persons' responses to climate change, racism, economic injustice, and threats to democracy.

Sadly, religion has contributed to hopelessness, apathy, denial, and violence. The false doctrine of the datable, foreordained

---

33 Transcript: Greta Thunberg's Speech at the U.N. Climate Action Summit.

Second Coming of Jesus has mitigated responses to social injustice and climate change. Secretary of Interior James Watt , during Ronald Reagan's presidency, asserted, "We don't have to protect the environment, the Second Coming is at hand." If God will destroy the earth, why worry about this one? Another group of apocalyptic Second Coming Christians believe that "the bad news is the good news." Wars and rumors of war, violence and upheaval, are signs that Jesus is coming soon, and should inspire rejoicing. Other persons of faith hold views of divine predestination and the belief that God has already ordained the future of the planet and our nation, God has predetermined peoples' social standing, and there is nothing we can do about it. God ordains the status quo. Our political protests may be an affront to God's predetermined future, related to persons and the planet.

Process prophetic faith contrasts with theological and political hopelessness and prevarication of our planet's leaders and many of their followers. Process thought realizes that God's aim is the best for this impasse, personally and planetarily, and that the best may not be pleasant. It may even involve God's confrontational attempts to mitigate destruction that has been put into motion by our values and actions. Process prophetic faith, however, believes that hope comes from agency, alignment with God's vision, and the reality that the future, though perilous, is still open to change. We can make a difference! Radically changing our personal and political lives can significantly change the world to come, reconcile persons with one another, and heal our national divisions. God calls us to creative transformation that transfigures and heals the world. When we align ourselves with God's vision, we plant seeds of God's realm "on earth as it is in heaven" and thus become God's partners in healing the earth.

Is it too late for the United States, for democracy, for reconciliation, and for the planet? Prophets don't always succeed, but they have faith in the great "perhaps," the divine perhaps and on that the future depends. Follow me, God calls through the words of the prophets, claim my vision, a new world is awaiting.

We conclude with prophetic images of hope. While must be realistic, and recognize the perils we face, without hope, the future is lost. As Harry Emerson Fosdick prays, "save us from weak resignation to the evils we deplore, let the gift of your salvation be our glory ever more."[34]

Hope is, as my wife Kate says, "a pick and shovel virtue." We must be imaginative; we must also do the hard work of hope-bringing. Take time for quiet contemplation. What gives you hope? For yourself? For your nation? For the planet? What are the impediments to hope?

Focus on one or two images of hope, praying that God grant you "wisdom and courage for the living of these days." How might these personal, communal, national, or planetary images be incarnate in our world?

Prayerfully considering your agency in changing the world, what is God calling you to do bring these images of hope to fruition?

Conclude by praying for guidance, energy, and courage to be a prophetic hope-giver and hope-liver.

---

34 Harry Emerson Fosdick, "God of Grace and God of Glory."

Prophetic Texts

Karen Baker-Fletcher, *Dancing with God: The Trinity from a Womanist Perspective* (Chalice, 2006).

Walter Brueggemann, *The Prophetic Imagination* (Fortress, 2018, 1978).

John Cobb, *Is It Too Late? A Theology of Ecology* (Fortress, 2021, 1971).

Monica Coleman, *Making a Way of No Way: A Womanist Theology* (Fortress, 2008).

Bruce Epperly, *Process Theology: Embracing Adventure with God* (Energion, 2014).

Bruce Epperly, *Process Theology and Healing* (Energion, 2023).

Bruce Epperly, *Process Theology and Mysticism* (Energion, 2023).

Bruce Epperly, *Talking Politics with Jesus: A Process Perspective on the Sermon on the Mount,* Energion, 2022.

Pope Francis, *Laudato Si! Our Common Home* (Our Sunday Visitor, 2015).

David Griffin, *Protecting Our Common, Sacred Home: Pope Francis and Process Theology* (Process Century Press, 2016).

Abraham Joshua Heschel, *The Prophets* (Harper, 1962).

Schubert Ogden, *Faith and Freedom: A Theology of Liberation* (Wipf and Stock, 2005).

Larry Rasmussen, *Earth-Honoring Faith: Ethics in a New Key* (Oxford, 2015).

Dorothe Sölle, *The Silent Cry: Mysticism and Resistance,* (Fortress Press, 2001).

Howard Thurman, *Jesus and the Disinherited* (Beacon Press, 1996).

www.ingramcontent.com/pod-product-compliance
Lightning Source LLC
Chambersburg PA
CBHW010039040426
42331CB00037B/3321